Lions

Ranters, Ravers and Rhymers

As a Cambridge undergraduate, Farrukh Dhondy was involved with Carcanet poetry magazine and the publication of poetry from new voices. Now a leading writer and commentator on multi-cultural issues, he has chosen for this anthology poems from Caribbean, African, Indian and black British poets which use the English language in startlingly innovative ways – from reggae lyrics, calypso and dub poetry to the measured ironies of Indian poets such as Eunice de Souza and Arun Kolatkar.

Acknowledgements

The publishers gratefully acknowledge permission to reprint copyright material to the following:

Heinemann Publishers Ltd for **Public Execution in Pictures** from *Beware Soul Brother* by Chinua Achebe. John Agard and the Caroline Sheldon Literary Agency for **Limbo Dancer at Immigration** and **Look** from *Limbo Dancer in Dark Glasses*. James Berry for **Caribbean Proverb Poems 1 & 2**. Oxford University Press for **On an Afternoon Train from Purley to Victoria, 1955** from *Chain of Days* by James Berry. Race Today Publications for **Natural High, Riddym Ravings, School Days, Dry** and **Simple Tings** by Jean Binta Breeze from *Riddym Ravings and Other Poems* (ed. Mervyn Morris). Heinemann Publishers Ltd and Dennis Brutus for **The Sun on This Rubble** and **Poems about Prison 1 – Cold**. Chatto & Windus Ltd for **Mama Dot I, Mama Dot II** and **Oracle Mama Dot** by Fred D'Aguiar from *Mama Dot*. Eunice de Souza and Newground for **Mrs Hermione Gonsalvez, Sweet Sixteen** and **Feeding the Poor at Christmas** by Eunice de Souza from *Fix*. Eunice De Souza and Praxis for **Encounter at a London Party** and **Meeting Poets** from *Women in Dutch Painting*. Oxford University Press, India, for **Ganga, Background, Casually** and **How the English Lessons Ended** by Nissim Ezekiel from *Hymns in Darkness*. Mahmood Jamal for **The Way You Loved Me** and **A Peasant in Bengal** by Mamood Jamal. Adil Jussawalla for **Approaching Santa Cruz Airport, Bombay** and **Karata**. Penumbra Productions Ltd for **An Old Woman** and **Ajamil and the Tigers** by Arun Kolatkar from *Jejuri*. Race Today Publications for **Inglan is a Bitch** and **Di Black Petty-Booshwah** from *Inglan is a Bitch*. Richard S. Mabala and the University of Dar es Salaam for **Turn-Boy** by Richard S. Mabala. Mambo Press for **Th' Anniversary** and **The Future A Mad Poem** by Dambudzo Marechera from *Patterns of Poetry in Zimbabwe* by Flora Wild. E. A. Markham for **West Indian Myth 2** and **The Boy of the House** by E. A. Markham. Island Music Ltd for **No Woman No Cry** by Bob Marley. Oxford University Press, India, for **A Letter to a Friend** by Arvind Krishna Mehotra from *Middle Earth*. Penguin Books (India) Ltd, for **Jason** and **Gone Away** by Dom Moraes from *Collected Poems by Dom Moraes*. Penumbra Productions Ltd for **The Street He Lives In** and **For Future Reference** by H. O. Nazareth. Virago Press for **With Apologies to Hamlet, Granny, Granny, Please Comb My Hair, On Receiving a Jamaican Postcard**, and **Love** by Grace Nichols from *Lazy Thoughts of a Lazy Woman*. University of South Africa, Pretoria, for **Letter from Pretoria Central Prison** by Arthur Nortje from *Dead Roots* (Heinemann 1973). Ijala Press for **Dreamtime 5 and 8** by Femi Oyebode from *Naked to Your Softness and Other Dreams*. Oxford University Press, India, for **Servants** from *Poems, 1966*, and **On Killing a Tree** by Gieve Patel from *Ten Twentieth Century Indian Poets* (ed. R. Parthasarathy). Oxford University Press, India, for **Obituary** from *Selected Poems* by A. K. Ramanujan. Mambo Press for **Harsh Noises** and **A Child's Cry** by Kristina Rungano from *Patterns of Poetry in Zimbabwe* by Flora Wild. University of Pittsburgh Press for **Uncle Time** from *Uncle Time* by Dennis Scott. Race Today Publications for **I an I Alone, Me Feel It, Yuh See**, and **Black and White** from *It a Come: Poems by Michael Smith*. Wole Soyinka for **Telephone Conversation** by Wole Soyinka. Farrar, Straus & Giroux, Inc. and Faber & Faber Ltd for **The Spoiler's Return** by Derek Walcott from *The Fortunate Traveller*. Longman Zimbabwe for **You Were** from *Kingfisher, Jikinya and Other Poems* by Musaemura Bonas Zimunya. Longman Group UK for **Kisimiso** from *Thought Tracks* by Musaemura Bonas Zimunya.

Every effort has been made to trace the owners of the copyright material in this book. In the event of any questions arising as to the use of any material, the editor will be pleased to make the necessary corrections in future editions of the book.

Farrukh Dhondy (Ed.)

Ranters, Ravers, and Rhymers

Poems by Black and Asian Poets

Lions
An Imprint of HarperCollinsPublishers

Other Lions poetry books

Mother Gave a Shout
Poems by Women and Girls
ed. *Susanna Steele and Morag Styles*

Is That the New Moon?
Poems by Women Poets
ed. *Wendy Cope*

The Hypnotiser
and other skyfoogling poems
by *Michael Rosen*

First published in Great Britain by HarperCollins 1990
First published in Lions 1992
Second impression July 1992

Lions is an imprint of HarperCollins Children's Books,
a division of HarperCollins Publishers Ltd,
77–85 Fulham Palace Road, Hammersmith,
London W6 8JB

ISBN 0-00-673748-4

Set in Bembo
Printed and bound in Great Britain by
HarperCollins Manufacturing, Glasgow

CONTENTS

THE CARIBBEAN

INDIA

AFRICA

INTRODUCTION

Even though this collection of poems is called *Ranters, Ravers and Rhymers*, it would take a bolder person than this editor to separate them under those headings and say which is which. To my list of three Rs I could have added a fourth — "revolutionaries" — and been sure that some of the poets and lyricists gathered here would be proud of being classed as such.

I have divided my chosen poets geographically: black poets who live and write in Britain, poets from the Caribbean, from India and from Africa.

Their poems share one very general thing in common. They could not, in my opinion, have been written by a Britisher or by a white American. There is a particularity about their subject matter which sets them apart. Very many of the poems can be seen as coming to terms with speaking verse in English, others can be seen as coming to terms with a world divided into the "first" and "third" categories.

For the purpose of this collection, "black" is a convenient term. The British left their language in all their ex-colonies including America. There is no doubt now that there is English literature and there is American literature. No doubt either that there is a black American literature with its own history and several dominant concerns and important voices. So many that this collection, in my opinion, couldn't tackle them. They would need a separate book by themselves, especially as in my Caribbean section I have included the lyrics of Bob Marley and David Rudder as examples of a particular sort of rhyming, raving and revolution. If I had included the American blacks I would have had to represent here, apart from the verse written as verse to be read on the page, an historical collection of blues, of jazz lyrics, of rock and roll, of gospel and soul.

From Africa and from the Indian subcontinent I've had to make a ruthless choice. No poets who write in languages other than English are included, though there are hundreds. In Pakistan, India and Bangladesh there are forty or more literary traditions – there's Urdu poetry, Bengali poetry, Tamil poetry and so on. I have only chosen here a completely unrepresentative sample of poets who write as though their first language was English. Similarly with Africa and the Caribbean, I have not included poets who write in French or poets who write in Swahili or Yoruba. I have no poets from Spanish-speaking Cuba or from Dutch Surinam.

In this collection I have called a lot of poets who live in Britain, mostly in London, "black British". They may not like this but they are stuck with it because their first audiences, at least for their mature published work, were British. Their work is, in some poems, a reaction to being in Britain and in a few poems it adopts the perspective of someone who has come away from a "home" elsewhere to the land of the birth of English.

Some black poets have expressed the view that the experience of colonialism and slavery which their nations suffered has "stolen their original tongues". This collection of poems in English by black and Asian poets gathers together the expressions of the new "English" tongues that have grown in place of the stolen ones.

English was born anew, without dying first, in several parts of the globe. Some poems in the collection are distinctly in these different forms of English, the English spoken by Jamaicans or by Nigerians. Very many of the poets don't write in these forms and attempt instead to renew the way complex poetic English has been written in the twentieth century in the main English tradition.

Some of the poems in this collection sing, and you can read them as though you were listening to a catchy tune. Others speak to you and urge you to think, to meditate on an atmosphere or a feeling. Some of them tell whole stories or the fragments of a story. Critics call these sorts of poems all manner of different names: runic, confessional, meditative, public. What poetry means to me is the recruitment of experience into the discipline of words.

In a way this collection follows a pattern of personal awareness. This is the best sense in which it can be my personal collection. While growing up in India, I thought all poetry in English was written by English people or by Americans. The idea of Indian poetry in English didn't exist. Sure, there were "poems" in our school magazine and later in the university and college student magazines, but they were the product, I always believed, of imposters. The first poet I met from my own world was Adil Jussawalla. Here was a young man who wanted to write poetry, having already spent a year at Oxford, who assumed that his voice was as eligible as those of the published poets of Britain whose work one encountered in magazines and books. Then there was Dom Moraes and there was Nissim Ezekiel. There followed an awareness of an anthill of poetic activity — busy, close to the ground, burrowing at times and capable of a sting or two.

I came to England. There was no "black" poetry here at the time (the mid-Sixties). Then came the era of black American publication, not verse but prose: the explosive, provocative, defiant writing of George Jackson, Malcolm X, Eldridge Cleaver, Bobby Seale and Angela Davis. No poetry (at least, not published in Britain), but a literature that seemed to lay tracks along which poetic feeling could follow. The one thing these writers gave the world was the definition of a black voice. Then there was no looking back.

At first this collection may seem to the reader or to the critic a curious one. Maybe my justification may make it seem curiouser. I wanted to gather together, from the poets I personally find enjoyable, those that I feel will be accessible to young people. That leaves out, for instance, huge chunks of the work of Derek Walcott, whose poetry is difficult, and most of the poetry of a poet such as Adil Jussawalla, who works in territories of experience and emotion which are distinctly more adult. (When I was a teenager, of course, being told precisely that would make me want to read all of Walcott and Jussawalla. Good luck!)

I have not included poems which deal in broad generalities but have included those which start in observation, of oneself or of things outside oneself. I have also tried to avoid the distinction between oral and written poetry. There is no doubt that Bob Marley's lyrics, for example, are weaker on the page than the rhythms of "written" poems and need melody and orchestration as accompaniments to their meaning. Nevertheless, one can't leave the most important movement in popular song out of a collection which is primarily meant to be read for kicks and also meant to lead the reader to other poems by the same poets.

I suppose an anthologer feels like the host at a party at which the reader is the chief guest. You invite those whom your chief guest should meet: you hope that he or she will get acquainted and maybe make dates with one or two.

FARRUKH DHONDY
June 1990

Black Britain

JOHN AGARD

Limbo Dancer at Immigration

It was always the same
at every border/at every frontier/
at every port/at every airport/
　　　　　of every metropolis

The same hassle
from authorities

the same battle
with bureaucrats

a bunch of official cats
ready to scratch

looking limbo dancer up & down
scrutinising passport with a frown

COUNTRY OF ORIGIN: SLAVESHIP

Never heard of that one
the authorities sniggered

Suppose you got here on a banana boat
the authorities sniggered

More likely a spaceship
the authorities sniggered

Slaveship/spaceship/Pan Am/British Airways/
   Air France
It's all the same
smiled limbo dancer

Now don't give us any of your lip
the authorities sniggered

ANY IDENTIFYING MARKS?

And when limbo dancer showed them sparks
of vision in eyes that held rivers
            it meant nothing to them

And when limbo dancer held up hands
that told a tale of nails
            it meant nothing to them

And when limbo dancer offered a neck
that bore the brunt of countless lynchings
            it meant nothing to them

And when limbo dancer revealed ankles
bruised with the memory of chains
            it meant nothing to them

So limbo dancer bent over backwards
            & danced
            & danced
            & danced

until from every limb
flowed a trail of red

& what the authorities thought
was a trail of blood

was only spilt duty-free wine

so limbo dancer smiled
saying I have nothing to declare

& to the sound of drum disappeared

JOHN AGARD

Look

Do not look for limbo dancer
in nightclubs of Port of Spain/or Montego Bay
for there you'll find only limbo dancer's shadow

look among the masses
joining endless queues for bread
for limbo dancer/has known the urgency/of
    hunger

look for that body bent like a bow
among the vigil for the New Cross dead

for limbo dancer/knows too well/the joys of
    parenthood
trapped/screaming fire/a living hell

look for those limbs linked like song
to 30,000 voices of women at Greenham
    Common

for limbo dancer cherishes the bloom of
    sisterhood/
& remembers well the pain of rape/a slaveship
    womb
like unwanted missile

look for the arching neck
among the children of Soweto
& the miners of Gdansk

for limbo dancer has known the rupture of
    brotherhood
herded together/eyes washed in blood

wherever sisterhood & brotherhood join in
    struggle
there you will find a rainbow of protest

JAMES BERRY

Caribbean Proverb Poems 1

Dog mornin prayer is, Laard,
wha teday, a bone or a blow?

Tiger wahn to eat a child, tiger sey
he could-a swear it was a puss.

If yu cahn mek plenty eyewater
fo funeral, start a-bawl early mornin.

Caribbean Proverb Poems 2

1
Hungrybelly an Fullbelly
dohn walk same pass.

Fullbelly always a-tell Emptybelly
"Keep heart".

2
Yu fraid of eye
yu cahn eat cowhead.

Eye meet eye
an man fraid!

3
Yu see yu neighbour beard
on fire, yu tek water
and wet yu own.

When lonely man dead,
grass come grow a him door.

4
Satan may be ol
but Satan not bedriddn.

Man who is all honey,
fly dem goin eat him up.

JAMES BERRY

On an Afternoon Train from Purley to Victoria, 1955

Hello, she said and startled me.
Nice day. Nice day I agreed.
I am a Quaker she said and Sunday
I was moved in silence
to speak a poem loudly
for racial brotherhood.

I was thoughtful, then said
what poem came on like that?
One the moment inspired she said.
I was again thoughtful.

Inexplicably I saw
empty city streets lit dimly
in a day's first hours.
Alongside in darkness
was my father's big banana field.

Where are you from? she said.
Jamaica I said.
What part of Africa is Jamaica? she said.
Where Ireland is near Lapland I said.
Hard to see why you leave
such sunny country she said.
Snow falls elsewhere I said.

So sincere she was beautiful
as people sat down around us.

FRED D'AGUIAR

Mama Dot I

Born on a sunday
in the kingdom of Ashante

Sold on monday
into slavery

Ran away on tuesday
cause she born free

Lost a foot on wednesday
when they catch she

Worked all thursday
till her head grey

Dropped on friday
where they burned she

Freed on saturday
in a new century

FRED D'AGUIAR

Mama Dot II

Old Mama Dot
old Mama Dot
boss a de stew-pot
she nah deal in vat
she nah bap
no style
so stop
look at Mama Dot
windin on de spot

Old Mama Dot
old Mama Dot
watch her squat
full o de nat-
-tral goodness dat
grow in de lann
she use to farm
bare hann
up evry dawn

Old Mama Dot
old Mama Dot
she nah deal wid vat-
-igan nah mek no fuss
she a deal wid duss
she swing cutlass
play big boss
lick chile rass
go to mass

FRED D'AGUIAR

Oracle Mama Dot

I am seated at her bare feet.
The rocking chair on floorboards
Of the verandah is the repeated break
Of bracken underfoot. *Where are we heading?*

Who dare speak in these moments before dark?
The firefly threads its infinite morse;
Crapauds and crickets are a mounting cacophony;
The laughter of daredevil bats.

Dusk thickens into night.
She has rocked and rocked herself to sleep.
She may hold silence for another millennium.
I see the first stars among cloud.

MAHMOOD JAMAL

The Way You Loved Me

The way you loved me
was a lesson in subversion
and the way I loved you
a consolidation of power.

Staring emptily over the wall
is all that is left of our dream
as broken words trip over the wires
and turn to screams;
the smile becomes an intruder's body
twisted by machine-gun fire.

Only if we could
kill each other's fears
instead of slaying our hopes
from day to day!
So that everything you say
becomes a statement of our struggle
and everything I do defies our separation.

But then again
all this is hardly possible;
in the dim light of our thoughts
contradictions and suspicions multiply.
And we wait for night time
to send us down the streets again

in search of each other.

MAHMOOD JAMAL

A Peasant in Bengal

My first son died
when the cyclone struck.
I found his bone in the rubble.
Here it is under my pillow;
it talks to me when I am lonely.

My second son
drowned in the floods.
I have his shirt to remind me;
it smells of my own sweat.

My wife died
giving birth to my third son.
They brought him back
torn with bullets.
I have no reminders of him;
only the rattle of machine guns
across the river.

LINTON KWESI JOHNSON

Di Black Petty-Booshwah
(for Railton Youth Club members)

dem wi' gi' whey dem talent to di State
an' di black workin' class andahrate
dem wi' side wid oppressah
w'en di goin' get ruff
side wid aggressah
w'en di goin' get tuff

dem a black petty-booshwah
dem full a flaw
an' dem a black petty-booshwah
dem full a flaw

tru dem seh dem edicate dem a gwaan irate
tru dem seh dem edicate dem a seek tap rate
dem a seek posishan
aaf di backs af blacks
seek promoshan
aaf di backs af blacks

dem a black petty-booshwah
dem full a flaw
an' dem a black petty-booshwah
dem full a flaw

dem a run-up dem mout' an' a shout all about
tru dem have a lat a dou't 'bout di stren't af blacks
dem a run-up dem mout'
an' a shout all about

but w'en wi launch wi attack
dem wi' haffi dress back

dem a black petty-booshwah
dem full a flaw
an' dem a black petty-booshwah
dem full a flaw!

LINTON KWESI JOHNSON

Inglan is a Bitch

w'en mi jus' come to Landan toun
mi use to work pan di andahgroun
but workin' pan di andahgroun
y'u don't get fi know your way aroun'

Inglan is a bitch
dere's no escapin' it
Inglan is a bitch
dere's no runnin' whey fram it

mi get a lickle jab in a big 'otell
an' awftah a while, mi woz doin' quite well
dem staat mi aaf as a dish-washah
but w'en mi tek a stack, mi noh tun clack-
    watchah!

Inglan is a bitch
dere's no escapin' it
Inglan is a bitch

noh baddah try fi hide fram it

w'en dem gi' you di lickle wage packit
fus dem rab it wid dem big tax rackit
y'u haffi struggle fi mek en's meet
an' w'en y'u goh a y'u bed y'u jus' cant sleep

Inglan is a bitch
dere's no escapin' it
Inglan is a bitch fi true
a noh lie mi a tell, a true

mi use to work dig ditch w'en it cowl noh bitch
mi did strang like a mule, but, bwoy, mi did fool
den awftah a while mi jus' stap dhu ovahtime
den awftah a while mi jus' phu dung mi tool

Inglan is a bitch
dere's no escapin' it
Inglan is a bitch
y'u haffi know how fi suvvive in it

well mi dhu day wok an' mi dhu nite wok
mi dhu clean wok an' mi dhu dutty wok
dem seh dat black man is very lazy
but if y'u si how mi wok y'u woulda sey mi crazy

Inglan is a bitch
dere's no escapin' it
Inglan is a bitch
y'u bettah face up to it

dem have a lickle facktri up inna a Brackly
inna disya facktri all dem dhu is pack crackry
fi di laas fifteen years dem get mi laybah
now awftah fifteen years mi fall out a fayvah

Inglan is a bitch
dere's no escapin' it
Inglan is a bitch
dere's no runnin' whey fram it

mi know dem have work, work in abundant
yet still, dem mek mi redundant
now, at fifty-five mi gettin' quite ol'
yet still, dem sen' mi fi goh draw dole

Inglan is a bitch
dere's no escapin' it
Inglan is a bitch fi true
is whey wi a goh dhu 'bout it?

E. A. MARKHAM

West Indian Myth 2

We don't sing Brother, we don't play the coon
We storm the fort with intellect, with dialectic
   cool.

International travellers, we smash the native
   barrier
With skill and flexibility of the licensed degree-
   carrier.

We spread the word in approved tongues and
   helpful thighs
For we are your alternative to hypocrisies,
   jealousies and lies:

We're not your common, vulgar, phrase-book
   sort
We bring you Mao, Marcuse — even J.-P. Sartre
   on Art.

So when the show is over and Madame invites to
   disrobe her
"he who could greet you in Swahili and say
   goodbye in Yoruba",

How dare the upstart, "Power to Baader-
   Meinhof" louts
The "ça va, ça va, alle ist klar, baby, alle ist klar"
   touts

Jump the queue and leave you scrambling for the
    dictionary
Like a twopenny–ha'penny, centime, pfennig
    nobody.

E. A. MARKHAM

The Boy of the House

The ruin of the house, he lies on his stomach,
    womanless.
The boy is in water, frog-like, his mouth tastes of
    seaweed.
He is looking at the rose garden, it's not there
No longer at the front of the house —
Of what used to be the house . . .

The rose garden is now at the bottom of the sea
And the boy throws a line, then another
To prevent more of the house drifting away.
He does this instead of growing into middle age,
    or going abroad:
The boy is a great source of worry.

H. O. NAZARETH

The Street He Lives In

He's lived eleven years, today, on one
side or the other of this street, without
getting domesticated like the mass
of his contemporaries everywhere.

Arriving confident, naive, he found
a flat most memorable for marks left
by former tenants on the floor and walls.
Furnishings shammed the spirit of that word,
the landlord swallowed, weekly, rants and rent.

The North Star, at the top, on Finchley Road,
each evening hummed: a hub for immigrants,
hangers–on, and hookers of both sexes.
Most left. They moved, or bought suburban
    homes,
found better pubs and pickings somewhere else,
got bored with the newcomers, or were barred.
Since damaged by a bomb in December
1974, the place is flush
with dolly–birds and dolled–up boys as square
as the new plush and dimly–lit decor.

The property developers edged out
wage–earning families from this once cos-
mopolitan ward bordering on the real
estate of Hampstead; left it dying, owned
by junior exec. types, and lesser–known
exponents of the arts; turned over oil–

rich foreign leasers here on spending sprees;
and pointing forward to a bureaucrat-
ic heyday, got tenants like him, staying
put, to crawl into the woodwork of lately
purchased, furbished council property.

On the other side, "County" Kilburn's com-
promised by black and tan, reggae-loving
West Indians, and Kenyan Asian grocers.
Some work-worn navvies still regard
weekends as alcoholidays — exchange
frustration's words and blows among
   themselves,
but without sense or malice — though a few,
cold with outrage at the plight of Ireland,
bomb buildings put up elsewhere, possibly
by their compatriots, creating work,
fear, and injudicious indignation.

Brown leaves, naked branches, spring buds,
   summer
foliage, inform redbrick of the seasons.
The street itself remains strictly one-way —
dormitory for cars and weekday beeline
for harried folks in vehicles that go
horny watching dustcart peepshows, milk-float
mammaries, and lorries' inviting rumps.
Sweet-do-nothing on Sunday only.

H. O. NAZARETH

For Future Reference

When he feels old
and something of a failure,
(saying, "Life was good though",
and saying, "Not much I could do")
and the sun insists on being brilliant,
Lobo contemplates dying, poetry,
and the kitchen table too.

He marvels that life should seem so barren
since he accepts that it's a bit absurd,
saying, "Theists have ultimates to tease them",
and saying, "Why didn't I join a guerilla gang?"
He turns the radio on — an opera —
the music's youthful, the words
are sensual, but something's wrong.

He knows he's stuck in London
though he'd like to return to where he came
    from,
saying, "At least I've got a job and a flat here",
and saying, "The entertainment's better",
not having even seen a film in the past few
    months.
He thinks of people he has loved
and wonders what happened to him, or her.

Then he gets nostalgic
and thinks, maybe things are not that bad,
saying, "I'm still young too",
and saying, "Just a state I'm going through —
didn't get much sleep these last few days".
He flexes his muscles tentatively,
considers what it's really like being thirty-two.

GRACE NICHOLS

With Apologies to Hamlet

To pee or not to pee
That is the question

Whether it's sensibler in the mind
To suffer for sake of verse
The discomforting slings
Of a full and pressing bladder
Or to break poetic thought for loo
As a course of matter
And by apee-sing end it.

GRACE NICHOLS

Love

Love is not a grindstone
constantly grinding
wearing down to bone

Love is not an interlocking
deadlock
of inseparable flesh
or a merging of metals
to smooth alloy

Love is a sunshawl
that keeps the beloved warm

Even the undeserving
love floods
risking all.

GRACE NICHOLS

On Receiving a Jamaican Postcard

Colourful native entertainers
dancing at de edge of de sea
a man-an-woman combination
choreographing
de dream of de tourist industry

de two a dem in smiling conspiracy
to capture dis dream of de tourist industry

an de sea blue
an de sky blue
an de sand gold fuh true

an de sea blue
an de sky blue
an de sand gold fuh true

He staging a dance-prance
head in a red band
beating he waist drum
as if he want to drown she wid sound
an yes, he muscle looking strong

She a vision of frilly red
back-backing to he riddum
exposing she brown leg
arcing like lil mo
she will limbo into de sea

Anything fuh de sake of de tourist industry
Anything fuh de sake of de tourist industry

GRACE NICHOLS

Granny, Granny, Please Comb My Hair

Granny Granny please comb
my hair
you always take your time
you always take such care

You put me on a cushion
between your knees
you rub a little coconut oil
parting gentle as a breeze

Mummy Mummy
she's always in a hurry-hurry
rush
she pulls my hair
sometimes she tugs

But Granny
you have all the time
in the world
and when you're finished
you always turn my head and say
"Now who's a nice girl?"

The Caribbean

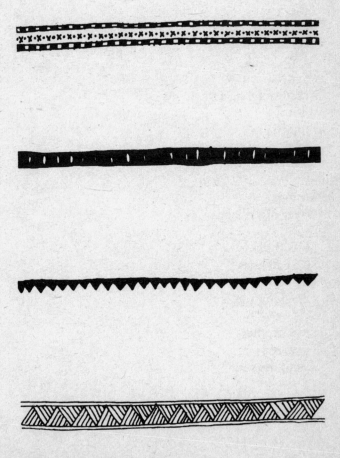

JEAN BINTA BREEZE

natural high

my mother is a
red
woman

she
gets high
on clean children

grows
common sense

injects
tales
with heroines

fumes
over dirty habits

hits the sky
on bad lines

cracking meteors

my mother
gets red
with the sun

JEAN BINTA BREEZE

simple tings
        (for Miss Adlyn and Aunt Vida)

de simple tings of life, mi dear
de simple tings of life

she rocked the rhythms in her chair
brushed a hand across her hair
miles of travel in her stare

de simple tings of life

ah hoe mi corn
an de backache gone
plant mi peas
arthritis ease

de simple tings of life

leaning back
she wiped an eye
read the rain signs
in the sky
evening's ashes
in a fireside

de simple tings of life

JEAN BINTA BREEZE

dry

(i)
from a standpipe in a tenement yard

days of
    dirty bundles
squatted
    by a cistern
altar

swollen feet
    clawed on cracks
  in the hot gutter

    lizard eyes
   of women
  fixed in worship
    on the mouth
of god
    which coughed its
     chronic lumps
    of air
begging them for
    water

(ii)

back to a standpipe in a tenement yard

we set drums
to catch the rain

it didn't rain
we trekked miles
to the river

the river dried
the trucks came
once or twice

then stopped

we marched
to see the councillor

who told us "sorry
my party's not
in power"

JEAN BINTA BREEZE

school days

one day
the school bus
missed its turning
crushed our mate
against the gate
doctor gave us tablets
for our nerves

the school choir
sang
at the funeral
a man looked at me
like a ghost
he had heard it was
the brown–skinned one

JEAN BINTA BREEZE

riddym ravings (the mad woman's poem)

de fus time dem kar me go a Bellevue
was fit di dactar an de lanlord operate
an tek de radio outa mi head
troo dem sieze de bed
weh did a gi mi cancer
an mek mi talk to nobady
ah di same night wen dem trow mi out fi no pay
   de rent
mi haffi sleep outa door wid de Channel One
   riddym box
an de DJ fly up eena mi head
mi hear im a play seh

Eh, Eh,
no feel no way
town is a place dat ah really kean stay
dem kudda — ribbit mi han
eh — ribbit mi toe
mi waan go a country go look mango

fah wen hungry mek King Street pavement
bubble an dally in front a mi yeye
an mi foot start wanda falla fly
to de garbage pan eena de chinaman backlat
dem nearly chap aff mi han eena de butcha shap
fi de piece a ratten poke
ah de same time de mawga gal in front a mi
drap de laas piece a ripe banana
an mi — ben dung — pick i up — an nyam i

49

a dat time dem grab mi an kar mi back a Bellevue
dis time de dactar an de lanlord operate
an tek de radio plug outa mi head
den sen mi out, seh mi all right
but — as ah ketch back outa street
ah push een back de plug
an ah hear mi DJ still a play, seh

Eh, Eh,
no feel no way
town is a place dat ah really kean stay
dem kudda — ribbit mi han
eh — ribbit mi toe
mi waan go a country go look mango

Ha Haah . . . Haa

wen mi fus come a town
mi use to tell everybady "mawnin"
but as de likkle rosiness gawn outa mi face
nobady nah ansa mi
silence tun rags roun mi bady
in de mids a all de dead people dem
a bawl bout de caast of livin
an a ongle one ting tap mi fram go stark raving
    mad
a wen mi siddung eena Parade
a tear up newspaper fi talk to
sometime dem roll up
an tun eena one a Uncle But sweet saaf
yellow heart breadfruit
wid piece a roas saalfish side a i
an if likkle rain jus fall

mi get cocanat rundung fi eat i wid
same place side a weh de country bus dem pull
   out
an sometime mi a try board de bus
an de canductor bwoy a halla out seh
"dutty gal, kum affa de bus"
ah troo im no hear de riddym eena mi head
same as de tape weh de bus driva a play, seh

Eh, Eh,
no feel no way
town is a place dat ah really kean stay
dem kudda — ribbit mi han
eh — ribbit mi toe
mi waan go a country go look mango
so country bus, ah beg yuh
tek mi home
to de place, where I belang

an di dutty bway jus run mi aff

Well, dis mawnin, mi start out pon Spanish
   Town Road,
fah mi deh go walk go home a country
fah my granny use to tell mi how she walk fram
   wes
come a town
come sell food
an mi waan ketch home befo dem put de price
   pon i'
but mi kean go home dutty?
fah mi parents dem did sen mi out clean
Ah!

see wan stanpipe deh!
so mi strip aff all de crocus bag dem
an scrub unda mi armpit
fah mi hear de two mawga gal dem laas nite
a laugh an seh
who kudda breed smaddy like me?
a troo dem no know seh a pure nice man
weh drive car an have gun
visit my piazza all dem four o'clock a mawnin
no de likkle dutty bwoy dem weh mi see dem a
   go home
wid
but as mi feel de clear water pon mi bady
no grab dem grab mi
an is back eena Bellevue dem kar mi
seh mi mad an a bade naked a street
well dis time de dactar an de lanlord operate
an dem tek de whole radio fram outa mi head
but wen dem tink seh mi unda chloroform
dem put i dung careless
an wen dem gawn
mi tek de radio
an mi push i up eena mi belly
fi keep de baby company
fah even if mi nuh mek i
me waan my baby know dis yah riddym yah
fram before she bawn
hear de DJ a play, seh

Eh, Eh,
no feel no way
town is a place dat ah really kean stay
dem kudda — ribbit mi han
eh — ribbit mi toe
mi waan go a country go look mango

an same time
de dactar an de lanlord
trigger de electric shack
an mi hear de DJ vice bawl out, seh

Murther
Pull up Missa Operator!

LORNA GOODISON

My Last Poem

I once wrote poems
that emerged so fine
with a rough edge for honing
a soft cloth for polishing
and a houseproud eye
I'd pride myself in making them shine.
But in this false winter
with the real cold to come
no, this season's shift
there are no winters here,
well call it what you will but the cold time is here
with its memorial crosses to mark
my father's dying
and me wondering where next year will find me
in whose vineyard toiling,
I gave my son
to a kind woman to keep
and walked down through the valley
on my scarred feet,
across the river
and into the guilty town
in search of bread
but they had closed the bakery down,
so I returned and said child
there was no bread
I'll write you my last poem instead
my last poem is not my best
all things weaken towards the end.
O but it should be laid out

and chronicled, crazy like my life
with a place for all my several lives
daughter, sister, mistress, friend, warrior
wife
and a high holy ending for the blessed
one
me as mother to a man.
There should be a place for
messages and replies
you are too tightly bound, too whole
he said
I loosened my hair and I bled
now you send conflicting signals they said
divided I turned both ways and fled.
There should be a place for all this
but I'm almost at the end of my last poem
and I'm almost a full woman.
I warm my son's clothes
in this cold time
in the deep of my bosom
and I'm not afraid of love.
In fact, should it be
that these are false signals I'm receiving
and not a real unqualified ending
I'm going to keep the word love
and use it in my next poem.
I know it's just the wordsmith's failing
to forge a new metal to ring like its rhyme
but I'll keep its fool's gold
for you see it's always bought me time.
And if I write another poem
I'm going to use it
for it has always used me

and if I ever write another poem
I'm going to return that courtesy.

LORNA GOODISON

I am Becoming My Mother

Yellow/brown woman
fingers smelling always of onions

My mother raises rare blooms
and waters them with tea
her birth waters sang like rivers
my mother is now me

My mother had a linen dress
the colour of the sky
and stored lace and damask
tablecloths
to pull shame out of her eye.

I am becoming my mother
brown/yellow woman
fingers smelling always of onions.

LORNA GOODISON

Tightrope Walker

And I have been a tightrope walker all my life,
that is, tightrope walking has been my main
    occupation.
In between stints in sundry fraudulent circuses
I've worked at poetry, making pictures
or being a paid smart-arse.
Once I even tried my hand at cashiering,
couldn't balance the ledger though
but I was honest, always overpaid someone
and had to make up the shortfall myself.
But it was too firm on the ground
so I put on my fishnet tights
my iridescent kingfisher blue bathing-suit
chalked the soles of my slippers of pliable gold
    kid
and took to the ropes again.

It's a fine life, those uncontained moments
in the air
those nerve-stretched belly-bottom spasms
from here to there
and your receiver copping what
from the ground looks like
an innocent feel
as he steadies you safely on the far side.
But I broke both arms
and the side of my head once
and had multiple miscarriages from
falling flat on my back

so I'm on the ground most days now
except for this, the tightest walk of all.
I don my new costume of
marabou and flamingo feathers
and my shade of oyster juliet cap
with the discreet spangles
and inch towards you once or twice a week.
I have to make record time
you have to be home before dark
and the entire act is really a rehearsal
here in this empty tent with last night's
sawdust to buffer the wild in our talk
and the fat lady sunning herself outside
and listening for secrets in our laughter
and it's all done with safety nets, thank you
and no audience invited to the finest
performances of me and you
but it's my life and my last act
before our show closes down
and re-opens to a gaping public
at some other circus ground.

LORNA GOODISON

Nanny

My womb was sealed
with molten wax
of killer bees
for nothing should enter
nothing should leave
the state of perpetual siege
the condition of the warrior.

From then my whole body would quicken
at the birth of everyone of my people's children.
I was schooled in the green-giving ways
of the roots and vines
made accomplice to the healing acts
of Chainey root, fever grass & vervain.

My breasts flattened
settled unmoving against my chest
my movements ran equal
to the rhythms of the forest.

I could sense and sift
the footfall of men
from the animals
and smell danger
death's odour
in the wind's shift.

When my eyes rendered
light from the dark

my battle song opened
into a solitaire's moan
I became most knowing
and for ever alone.

And when my training was over
they circled my waist with pumpkin seeds
and dried okra, a traveller's jigida
and sold me to the traders
all my weapons within me.
I was sent, tell that to history.

When your sorrow obscures the skies
other women like me will rise.

LORNA GOODISON

For My Mother (May I Inherit Half Her Strength)

My mother loved my father
I write this as an absolute
in this my thirtieth year
the year to discard absolutes

She appeared, her fate disguised,
as a Sunday player in a cricket match,
he had ridden from a country
one hundred miles south of hers.

She tells me he dressed the part,
visiting dandy, maroon blazer
cream serge pants, seam like razor,
and the beret and the two–tone shoes.

My father stopped to speak to her sister,
till he looked and saw her by the oleander,
sure in the kingdom of my blue–eyed
    grandmother.
He never played the cricket match that day.

He wooed her with words and he won her.
He had nothing but words to woo her,
On a visit to distant Kingston he wrote,

"I stood on the corner of King Street and looked,
and not one woman in that town was lovely as
    you".

My mother was a child of the petite bourgeoisie
studying to be a teacher, she oiled her hands
to hold pens.
My father barely knew his father, his mother died
     young,
he was a boy who grew with his granny.

My mother's trousseau came by steamer through
     the snows of Montreal
where her sisters Alberta of the cheekbones and
     the
perennial Rose, combed Jewlit backstreets with
     French-turned names for Doris's wedding
     things.

Such a wedding Harvey River, Hanover, had
     never seen
Who anywhere had seen a veil fifteen chantilly
     yards long?
and a crêpe de chine dress with inlets of silk
     godettes
and a neck-line clasped with jewelled pins!

And on her wedding day she wept. For it was a
     brazen bride in those days who smiled.
And her bouquet looked for the world like a sheaf
     of wheat
against the unknown of her belly,
a sheaf of wheat backed by maidenhair fern,
     representing Harvey River
her face washed by something other than river
     water.

My father made one assertive move, he took the
   imported cherub down
from the heights of the cake and dropped it in the
   soft territory
between her breasts . . . and she cried.

When I came to know my mother many years
   later, I knew her as the figure
who sat at the first thing I learned to read:
   "SINGER", and she breast–fed
my brother while she sewed; and she taught us to
   read while she sewed and
she sat in judgement over all our disputes as she
   sewed.

She could work miracles, she would make a
   garment from a square of cloth
in a span that defied time. Or feed twenty people
   on a stew made from
fallen–from–the–head cabbage leaves and a carrot
   and a cho–cho and a palmful of meat.
And she rose early and sent us clean into the
   world and she went to bed in
the dark, for my father came in always last.

There is a place somewhere where my mother
   never took the younger ones
a country where my father with the always smile
my father whom all women loved, who had the
   perpetual quality of wonder
given only to a child . . . hurt his bride.

Even at his death there was this "Friend" who
     stood by her side,
but my mother is adamant that that has no place
     in the memory of
my father.

When he died, she sewed dark dresses for the
     women amongst us
and she summoned that walk, straight-backed,
     that she gave to us
and buried him dry-eyed.

Just that morning, weeks after
she stood delivering bananas from their skin
singing in that flat hill country voice

she fell down a note to the realisation that she did
not have to be brave, just this once
and she cried.

For her hands grown coarse with raising nine
     children
for her body for twenty years permanently fat
for the time she pawned her machine for my
     sister's Senior Cambridge fees
and for the pain she bore with the eyes of a queen

and she cried also because she loved him.

BOB MARLEY

No Woman No Cry

No woman no cry
No woman no cry
No woman no cry
No woman no cry
Cause I remember when we used to sit
in a government yard in Trenchtown
Observing the hypocrites
Mingle with the good people we meet
Good friends we have,
Oh, good friends we have lost
along the way
In this great future,
you can't forget your past.
So dry your tears, I seh.

No woman no cry
No woman no cry
Little darlin', don't shed no tears
No woman no cry
Said I remember when we used to sit
in the government yard in Trenchtown
And then Georgie would make the fire lights
I seh, log would burnin' thru the nights
Then we would cook cornmeal porridge
of which I'll share with you
My feet is my only carriage
and so I've got to push on thru,
Oh, while I'm gone,
Everything's gonna be all right

Everything's gonna be all right
No woman no cry
No woman no cry
I seh little darlin'
don't shed no tears
No woman no cry.

BOB MARLEY

Them Belly Full
(But We Hungry)

Them belly full but we hungry
A hungry mob is a angry mob
A rain a fall but the dirt it tough
A pot a cook but the food no 'nough
You're gonna dance to Jah music, dance,
We're gonna dance to Jah music, dance,
Forget your troubles and dance,
Forget your sorrows and dance,
Forget your sickness and dance,
Forget your weakness and dance

Cost of livin' gets so high
Rich and poor they start to cry
Now the weak must get strong
They say oh, what a tribulation
Them belly full but we hungry
A hungry mob is a angry mob
A rain a fall but the dirt it tough
A pot a cook but you no 'nough

We're gonna chuck to Jah music, chuckin'
We're chuckin' to Jah music, we're chuckin'
Belly full but them hungry,
A hungry mob is a angry mob
A rain a fall but the dirt it tough
A pot a cook but the food no 'nough
A hungry mob is a angry mob

DAVID RUDDER

Calypso Music

Can you hear a distant drum
Bouncing on the laughter
Of a melody

Yeh eh yeh eh

And does the rhythm tell you
      come come come come
Does your spirit do a dance
To this symphony

Yeh eh yeh eh

Does it tell that your heart is the fire
      Oh yeh
And does it tell you that your pain is a liar
      Oh yeh
Does it wash away all your ungodly
Well, are you ready for a brand new discovery?

Calypso, calypso oh oh
      calypso music
            Yeh eh, yeh eh
Calypso, calypso oh oh
      Calypso
A little dudung dudung dudung dung music
A little dudung dudung dudung dung
Singing woe yeh woe yeh woe yeh
      Calypso

Singing woe yeh woe yeh woe yeh
  Calypso
Ah say that I am the seed of the growling
  Tiger now
Ah got to sing
  Woe yeh woe yeh woe yeh
  Calypso

It is a living vibration
Rooted deep within
My Caribbean belly
Lyrics to make a politician cringe
Or turn a woman's body into jelly
  Shake it up, shake it up
It is a sweet soca music
  Calypso
They coulda never refuse it
  Calypso
It make you shake like a shango now
  Calypso
Why it is the shaking you don't know
  That's calypso

Calypso, calypso oh oh
  Calypso music
    Yeh eh yeh eh
Calypso, calypso oh oh
  Calypso
A little dudung dudung dudung dung music
A little dudung dudung dudung dung
Singing woe yeh woe yeh woe yeh

Calypso
Singing woe yeh woe yeh woe yeh
Calypso
Ah say that I am the seed of the seed of
Attila now
And like a honey
Ah got to sing
Woe yeh woe yeh woe yeh
Calypso
Oh oh oh oh yeh
Ah ah ah ah ha

I can still hear lions
Roar through Greenwich Village
While Executor kill them dead
As the ribbon drew
Lord Invader conquers Berlin
But their hearts this time
And Lord Kitchener make it
Old London feel so new
Beginner and Terror too
Fitzroy Coleman fingers dancing in the pan
Dancing on the pan
And when you think that he through
He ain't start nothing yet
Ain't start nothing yet
Carnegie Hall graced by the presence of
Sparrow
Oh oh oh
And when Slinger done with deh tail
Hear them shouting
Don't go Sparrow don't go
Why?
Calypso, calypso oh oh

Calypso music
*   Yeh eh yeh eh*
Calypso, calypso oh oh
*   Calypso*
A little dudung dudung dudung dung music
A little dudung dudung dudung dung
Singing woe yeh woe yeh woe yeh
*   Calypso*
Singing woe yeh woe yeh woe yeh
*   Calypso*
Ah say that I am the seed of the seed of
The Spoiler now
*   Ah want to fall*
Woe yeh woe yeh woe yeh
*   Calypso*
Ah want to rise
Ah want to rise

From the time the first bamboo cut
And we drag it down up in the
St Ann's Hills
From the day the first chantwelle leave
        the band
The real jamming start
And today we jamming still, still
Creating rhythms that could be deadly
        like Headley
Only this time
Is the lyric and the melody
Whe sending us all to the boundary
From the bongo drum to the role of the
Tassa
Well ever since Europe came

And she make Bassa, Bassa
We jamming it

Calypso, calypso oh oh
    Calypso music
       Yeh eh yeh eh
Calypso, calypso oh oh
    Calypso
A little dudung dudung dudung dung music
A little dudung dudung dudung dung
Singing woe yeh woe yeh woe yeh
    Calypso
Singing woe yeh woe yeh woe yeh
    Calypso
Singing woe yeh woe yeh woe yeh
    Calypso
Singing woe yeh woe yeh woe yeh
    Calypso
We going to sing it inna London
We going to sing it in America
    Yeah
We going to sing it in Africa
We going to sing it in Europe
    La calypso
    Yeah
We going to sing it in America
    Yeah calypso now now now
We are going to sing the calypso
    Yeah
C–A–L–Y–P–S–O calypso now
C–A–L–Y–P–S–O
Everybody sing
C–A–L–Y–P–S–O

DENNIS SCOTT

Uncle Time

Uncle Time is a ole, ole man . . .
All year long im wash im foot in de sea,
long, lazy years on de wet san'
an shake de coconut tree dem
quiet-like wid im sea-win' laughter,
scrapin away de lan' . . .

Uncle Time is a spider-man, cunnin an cool,
im tell yu: watch de hill an yu si mi.
Huhn! Fe yu yiye no quick enough fe si
how im move like mongoose; man, yu tink im
   fool?

Me Uncle Time smile black as sorrow;
im voice is sof as bamboo leaf
but Laard, me Uncle cruel.
When im play in de street
wid yu woman — watch im! By tomorrow
she dry as cane-fire, bitter as cassava;
an when im teach yu son, long after
yu walk wid stranger, an yu bread is grief.
Watch how im spin web roun yu house, an creep
inside; an when im touch yu, weep . . .

MICHAEL SMITH

Black and White

went to an all black school
with an all black name
all black principal
black teacher

graduated
with an all black concept

with our blackety blackety frustration
we did an all black march
with high black hopes
and an all black song

got a few solutions
not all black

went to a show
and saw our struggles
in black and white

Lawwwwwd have mercy

MICHAEL SMITH

I An I Alone

I an I alone
a trod through creation.
Babylon on I right, Babylon on I lef,
Babylon in front of I an Babylon behind I,
an I an I alone in the middle
like a Goliath wid a sling-shot.

"Ten cent a bundle fi me calaloo!
Yuh a buy calaloo, dread? Ten cent."

Everybody a try fi sell someting,
everybody a try fi grab someting,
everybody a try fi hustle someting,
everybody a try fi kill someting,

but ting an ting mus ring,
an only a few can sing
cause dem naw face de same sinting.

(Sung) *It's a hard road to travel*
        An a mighty long way to go.
        Jesus, me blessed saviour,
        will meet us on the journey home.

"Shoppin bag! Shoppin bag! Five cent fi one!"
"Green pepper! Thyme! Skellion an pimento!"
"Remember de Sabbath day, to keep it holy!
Six days shalt thou labour,
but on the seventh day shalt thou rest."

"Hi, mam, how much fi dah piece a yam deh?
"No, no dat; dat! Yes; dat!"
"Three dollars a poun, nice gentleman."
"Clear out! Oonoo country people too damn
  tief!"
"Like yuh mumma!"
"Fi-me mumma? Wha yuh know bout me
  mumma?"
"Look ya, a might push dis inna yuh!"
"Yuh lie! A woulda collar yuh!"
"Bruck it up! But, dread, cool down!"
"All right, cool down. Rastafari!"

De people-dem a teck everyting meck a muckle.
Dem a try fi hustle down de price
fi meck two ends meet,
de odder one a try fi push up de price
fi meck de picni backbone get sinting fi eat.
But two teet meet an dem a bark,
dem cyaan stan de pressure,
dem tired fi compete wid hog an dawg,
but dem mus aspire fi someting better
although dem dungle-heap ketch a fire.

Cyaan meck blood outa stone,
an cow never know de use a im tail
till fly teck it, but from dem born
dem a fan de fly of poverty from dem ass
for dem never have a tail fi cover it.

"Watch me, watch me, watch me!" — "Hey,
  handcart-bwoy,
mind yuh lick dung me picni-dem, yuh know!"

"Tief! Tief! Tief!" — "Whe im deh?
Look out, meck a bruck im friggin neck!"
"Im a one a de P-dem!"

Yuh see it? Zacky was me frien
but look how im life a go end?
Party politics play de trick
an it lick im dung
wid de big coocoomacca stick.

I an I alone
a trod through creation,
Babylon on me right, Babylon on me lef,
Babylon in front of I an Babylon behind I,
an I an I alone inna de middle
like a Goliath wid a sling-shot.

"Picni-dem a bawl,
rent to pay,
wife to obey,
but only Jesus know de way!
De meek shall inherit de earth
an de fulness thereof!"

But look what she inherit?
Six months pregnant, five mout fi feed,
an her man deh a jail, no bail.

"Cho, Roy, man! Let me go, no, man?
Me no want no man inna '81!"
"So wha happen? It was only '80
yuh did a teck man? Cho, Doris, man,
consider dis late application."

Dem waan meck love pon hungry belly
jus fi figet dis moment of poverty
but she mus get breed
an dem haffi go face dem calamity.

"Joshua did seh oonoo fi draw oonoo belt tight."
"Which belt, when me tripe a come through me
    mout?"
"What happen, sah, yuh get deliver? Yuh naw
    answer?"
"Hi, lady, yuh believe in socialism?"
"No, sah, me believe in social livin."

"Calaloo! Shoppin bag! Thyme!"
"Dinner mints! Cigarettes an Wrigley's!"
"Hi, Albert, which part Tiny?"
"Hi, sah, beg yuh a ten cent, no?"
"Meck yuh no leave de man alone?"
"Hi, sexy! Honey-bunch! Sugar-plum!"
"Dog-shit! Cow-shit!"

I an I alone
a trod through creation,
Babylon on I right, Babylon on I lef,
Babylon behind I an Babylon in front of I,
an I an I alone inna de middle
like a Goliath wid a sling-shot.

Lawd, a find a ten cent.
Lawd, we naw go get no sentance.

MICHAEL SMITH

Me Feel It, Yuh See

Me feel it, yuh see,
fi see so much yout out deh
under such a hell of a strain
till dem don't even know dem name.
Dem out deh, nuffer dan cigarette butt,
out a luck a look fi wuk,
tinkin dat freedom is a senseless dream,
an grip wid such feelin of hostility
dem woulda strangle a dawg fi get a bone
an devalue dem dignity.

Me feel it, yuh see,
fi see dat inna dis-ya concrete jungle
de yout no got nuttin to relate to.
Some tryin fi get close to Babylon
to pay dem rent
but de system
han down a crucial kind a judgement.
An tears will not satisfy I
to preserve a democrisy
whereby youtful lives pay de penalty
for politicians' irresponsibility
while dem intellectual pen dragon
a justify de dutty currydunction
dat I live pon like a little mampala man.

Me feel it, yuh see,
fi see dat dem twis justice an equality
till it no address I-an-I reality,

dat when yuh teck a stock
big man haffi a run back
fi hanker pon im ole-lady frock,
fi ketch up im stomach
dat stretch out like a hammock.
Me feel it, yuh see,
but anytime yuh see
de yout-man-dem stumble
doan tink dem fall.
Watch out!
Dem a plan fi meck yuh bawl!

DEREK WALCOTT

The Spoiler's Return

I sit high on this bridge in Laventille,
watching that city where I left no will
but my own conscience and rum-eaten wit,
and limers passing see me where I sit,
ghost in brown gaberdine, bones in a sack,
and bawl: "Ay, Spoiler, boy! When you come
   back?"
And those who bold don't feel they out of place
to peel my limeskin back, and see a face
with eyes as cold as a dead macajuel,
and if they still can talk, I answer: "Hell".
I have a room there where I keep a crown,
and Satan send me to check out this town.
Down there, that Hot Boy have a stereo
where, whole day, he does blast my caiso;
I beg him two weeks' leave and he send me
back up, not as no bedbug or no flea,
but in this limeskin hat and floccy suit,
to sing what I did always sing: the truth.
Tell Desperadoes when you reach the hill,
I decompose, but I composing still:

I going to bite them young ladies, partner,
like a hotdog or a hamburger
and if you thin, don't be in a fright
is only big fat women I going to bite.

The shark, racing the shadow of the shark
across clear coral rocks, does make them dark —
that is my premonition of the scene
of what passing over this Caribbean.
Is crab climbing crab-back, in a crab-quarrel,
and going round and round in the same barrel,
is sharks with shirt-jacs, sharks with well-pressed
   fins,
ripping we small fry off with razor grins;
nothing ain't change but colour and attire,
so back me up, Old Brigade of Satire,
back me up, Martial, Juvenal, and Pope
(to hang theirself I giving plenty rope),
join Spoiler's chorus, sing the song with me,
Lord Rochester, who praised the nimble flea:

Were I, who to my cost already am
One of those strange, prodigious creatures, Man,
A spirit free, to choose for my own share,
What case of flesh and blood I pleased to wear,
I hope when I die, after burial,
To come back as an insect or animal.

I see these islands and I feel to bawl,
"area of darkness" with V.S. Nightfall.

Lock off your tears, you casting pearls of grief
on a duck's back, a waxen dasheen leaf,
the slime crab's carapace is waterproof
and those with hearing aids turn off the truth,
and their dark glasses let you criticise
your own presumptuous image in their eyes.
Behind dark glasses is just hollow skull,

and black still poor, though black is beautiful.
So, crown and mitre me Bedbug the First —
the gift of mockery with which I'm cursed
is just a insect biting Fame behind,
a vermin swimming in a glass of wine,
that, dipped out with a finger, bound to bite
its saving host, ungrateful parasite,
whose sting, between the cleft arse and its seat,
reminds Authority man is just meat,
a moralist as mordant as the louse
that the good husband brings from the
   whorehouse,
the flea whose itch to make all Power wince,
will crash a fête, even at his life's expense,
and these pile up in lime pits by the heap,
daily, that our deliverers may sleep.
All those who promise free and just debate,
then blow up radicals to save the state,
who allow, in democracy's defence,
a parliament of spiked heads on a fence,
all you go bawl out, "Spoils, things ain't so bad".
This ain't the Dark Age, is just Trinidad,
is human nature, Spoiler, after all,
it ain't big genocide, is just bohbohl;
safe and conservative, 'fraid to take side,
they say that Rodney commit suicide,
is the same voices that, in the slave ship,
smile at their brothers, "Boy, is just the whip",
I free and easy, you see me have chain?
A little censorship can't cause no pain,
a little graft can't rot the human mind,
what sweet in goat-mouth sour in his behind.
So I sing with Attila, I sing with Commander,

what right in Guyana, right in Uganda.
The time could come, it can't be very long,
when they will jail calypso for picong,
for first comes television, then the press,
all in the name of Civic Righteousness;
it has been done before, all Power has
made the sky shit and maggots of the stars,
over these Romans lying on their backs,
the hookers swaying their enormous sacks,
until all language stinks, and the truth lies,
a mass for maggots and a fête for flies;
and, for a spineless thing, rumour can twist
into a style the local journalist —
as bland as a green coconut, his manner
routinely tart, his sources the Savannah
and all pretensions to a native art
reduced to giggles at the coconut cart,
where heads with reputations, in one slice,
are brought to earth, when they ain't eating nice;
and as for local Art, so it does go,
the audience have more talent than the show.
Is Carnival, straight Carnival that's all,
the beat is base, the melody bohbohl,
all Port of Spain is a twelve-thirty show,
some playing Kojak, some Fidel Castro,
some Rastamen, but, with or without locks,
to Spoiler is the same old khaki socks,
all Frederick Street stinking like a closed drain,
Hell is a city much like Port of Spain,
what the rain rots, the sun ripens some more,
all in due process and within the law,
as, like a sailor on a spending spree,
we blow our oil-bloated economy

on projects from here to eternity,
and Lord, the sunlit streets break Spoiler's heart,
to have natural gas and not to give a fart,
to see them line up, pitch–oil tin in hand:
each independent, oil-forsaken island,
like jeering at some scrunter with the blues,
while you lend him some need–a–half-sole shoes,
some begging bold as brass, some coming
      meeker,
but from Jamaica to poor Dominica
we make them know they begging, every loan
we send them is like blood squeezed out of stone,
and giving gives us back the right to laugh
that we couldn't see we own black people starve,
and, more we give, more we congratulate
we-self on our own self-sufficient state.
In all them project, all them Five-Year-Plan,
what happen to the Brotherhood of Man?
Around the time I dead it wasn't so,
we sang the Commonwealth of caiso,
we was in chains, but chains made us unite,
now who have, good for them, and who blight,
      blight;
my bread is bitterness, my wine is gall,
my chorus is the same: "I want to fall".
Oh, wheel of industry, check out your cogs!
Between the knee-high trash and khaki dogs
Arnold's Phoenician trader reach this far,
selling you half–dead batteries for your car,
the children of Tagore, in funeral shroud,
curry favor and chicken from the crowd;
as for the Creoles, check their house, and look,
you bust your brain before you find a book,

when Spoiler see all this, ain't he must bawl,
"area of darkness", with V.S. Nightfall?
Corbeaux like cardinals line the La Basse
in ecumenical patience while you pass
the Beetham Highway — Guard corruption's
    stench,
you bald, black justices of the High Bench —
and beyond them the firelit mangrove swamps,
ibises practising for postage stamps,
Lord, let me take a taxi South again
and hear, drumming across the Caroni Plain,
the tabla in the Indian half hour
when twilight fills the mud huts of the poor,
to hear the tattered flags of drying corn
rattle a sky from which all the gods gone,
their bleached flags of distress waving to me
from shacks, adrift like rafts on a green sea,
"Things ain't go change, they ain't go change at
    all",
to my old chorus: "Lord, I want to bawl".
The poor still poor, whatever arse they catch.
Look south from Laventille, and you can watch
the torn brown patches of the Central Plain
slowly restitched by needles of the rain,
and the frayed earth, crisscrossed like old bagasse,
spring to a cushiony quilt of emerald grass,
and who does sew and sow and patch the land?
The Indian. And whose villages turn sand?
The fishermen doomed to stitching the huge net
of the torn foam from Point to La Fillette.

One thing with Hell, at least it organise
in soaring circles, when any man dies

he must pass through them first, that is the style,
Jesus was down here for a little while,
cadaverous Dante, big-guts Rabelais,
all of them wave to Spoiler on their way.
Catch us in Satan tent, next carnival:
Lord Rochester, Quevedo, Juvenal,
Maestro, Martial, Pope, Dryden, Swift,
    Lord Byron,
the lords of irony, the Duke of Iron,
hotly contending for the monarchy
in couplets or the old re-minor key,
all those who gave earth's pompous carnival
fatigue, and groaned "O God, I feel to fall!"
all those whose anger for the poor on earth
made them weep with a laughter beyond mirth,
names wide as oceans when compared with mine
salted my songs, and gave me their high sign.
All you excuse me, Spoiler was in town;
you pass him straight, so now he gone back
    down.

India

EUNICE DE SOUZA

Meeting Poets

Meeting poets I am disconcerted sometimes
by the colour of their socks
the suspicion of a wig
the wasp in the voice
and an air, sometimes, of dankness.

Best to meet in poems:
cool speckled shells
in which one hears
a sad but distant sea.

EUNICE DE SOUZA

Encounter at a London Party

For a minute we stand blankly together.
You wonder in what language to speak to me,
offer a pickled onion on a stick instead.
You are young and perhaps forgetful
that the Empire lives
only in the pure vowel sounds I offer you
above the din.

EUNICE DE SOUZA

Sweet Sixteen

Well, you can't say
they didn't try.
Mamas never mentioned menses.
A nun screamed: You vulgar girl
don't say brassières
say bracelets.
She pinned paper sleeves
on to our sleeveless dresses.
The preacher thundered:
Never go with a man alone
Never alone
and even if you're engaged
only passionless kisses.

At sixteen, Phoebe asked me:
Can it happen when you're in a dance hall
I mean, you know what,
getting *preggers* and all that, *when*
you're dancing?
I, sixteen, assured her
you could.

EUNICE DE SOUZA

Feeding the Poor at Christmas

Every Christmas we feed the poor.
We arrive an hour late: poor dears,
like children waiting for a treat.
Bring your plates. Don't move.
Don't try turning up for more.
No. Even if you don't drink
you can't take your share
for your husband. Say thank you
and a rosary for us every evening.
No. Not a towel *and* a shirt,
even if they're old.
What's that you said?
You're a good man, Robert, yes,
beggars can't be, exactly.

EUNICE DE SOUZA

Mrs Hermione Gonsalvez

Mrs Hermione Gonsalvez says:
In the good old days
I had looks *and* colour
now I've got only colour
just look at my parents
how they married me to a dark man
on my own I wouldn't even have
looked at him. Once we were going
somewhere for a holiday and I went on
ahead my hubby was to come later
and there were lots of fair
Maharashtrian ladies there and they
all said Mrs Gonsalvez how fair and
beautiful you are your husband must be
so good-looking too but when Gonsalvez came
they all screamed
and ran inside their houses
thinking the devil had come.

NISSIM EZEKIEL

How the English Lessons Ended

My Muslim neighbour's daughter,
getting on to nineteen
but not yet matriculate,
wears a burkha when she leaves for school
a hundred yards away.

They've tried and tried
to get her married off,
but three successive years
the girl has failed in English.
Each time the father railed,

the mother fainted, fasted and abused,
then they thought of me, the English teacher
just next door. A little help
is all she needs, if you don't mind,
you know we are neighbours long long time.

I agree we are neighbours long long time.
Send the girl along, I'll see
what I can do. She comes, sheds her bhurka:
tall, thin, dark, with shifting eyes,
small face and heavy clouds of hair.

She's very serious — for ten minutes,
then she smiles, and smiles some more.
In half an hour she giggles, I learn,
giggling is what she's really good at,
with plenty of practice, not at home.

Friendly with my daughter
who's getting on to sixteen
and about to matriculate —
we haven't tried to get *her* married off —
she takes her home one day

and shows her pictures
in a certain kind of book.
My daughter tells my wife
who tells my mother
who tells me. I laugh it off.

She comes again, and suddenly
she knows I know. The English lessons
end abruptly. I've learnt enough, she claims.
She's learnt enough to say she's learnt enough.
The father rails, the mother fasts and abuses

but she will not return.
They probably decide I made advances,
and almost hint as much
to my poor mother, who's outraged.
There's gratitude for you, she says,

That girl will never get a husband!

A month later she was married.
Now she doesn't need that picture-book.

NISSIM EZEKIEL

Background, Casually

A poet-rascal-clown was born,
The frightened child who would not eat
Or sleep, a boy of meagre bone.
He never learnt to fly a kite,
His borrowed top refused to spin.

I went to Roman Catholic school,
A mugging Jew among the wolves.
They told me I had killed the Christ,
That year I won the scripture prize.
A Muslim sportsman boxed my ears.

I grew in terror of the strong
But undernourished Hindu lads,
Their prepositions always wrong,
Repelled me by passivity.
One noisy day I used a knife.

At home on Friday nights the prayers
Were said. My morals had declined.
I heard of Yoga and of Zen.
Could I, perhaps, be rabbi-saint?
The more I searched, the less I found.

Twenty-two: time to go abroad.
First, the decision, then a friend
To pay the fare. Philosophy,
Poverty and Poetry, three
Companions shared my basement room.

The London seasons passed me by.
I lay in bed two years alone,
And then a Woman came to tell
My willing ears I was the Son
Of Man. I knew that I had failed

In everything, a bitter thought.
So, in an English cargo-ship
Taking French guns and mortar shells
To Indo-China, scrubbed the decks,
And learned to laugh again at home.

How to feel it home, was the point.
Some reading had been done, but what
Had I observed, except my own
Exasperation? All Hindus are
Like that, my father used to say,

When someone talked too loudly, or
Knocked at the door like the Devil,
They hawked and spat. They sprawled around.
I prepared for the worst. Married,
Changed jobs, and saw myself a fool.

The song of my experience sung,
I knew that all was yet to sing.
My ancestors, among the castes,
Were aliens crushing seed for bread
(The hooded bullock made his rounds).

One among them fought and taught,
A Major bearing British arms.
He told my father sad stories
Of the Boer War. I dreamed that
Fierce men had bound my feet and hands.

The later dreams were all of words.
I did not know that words betray
But let the poems come, and lost
That grip on things the worldly prize.
I would not suffer that again.

I look about me now, and try
To formulate a plainer view:
The wise survive and serve — to play
The fool, to cash in on
The inner and the outer storms.

The Indian landscape sears my eyes.
I have become a part of it
To be observed by foreigners.
They say that I am singular,
Their letters overstate the case.

I have made my commitments now.
This is one: to stay where I am,
As others choose to give themselves
In some remote and backward place.
My backward place is where I am.

NISSIM EZEKIEL

Ganga

We pride ourselves
on generosity

to servants. The woman
who washes up, suspected

of prostitution,
is not dismissed.

She always gets
a cup of tea

preserved for her
from the previous evening,

and a chapatti, stale
but in good condition.

Once a year, an old
sari, and a blouse

for which we could
easily exchange a plate

or a cup and saucer.
Besides, she borrows

small coins for pan
or a sweet for her child.

She brings a smell with her
and leaves it behind her,

but we are used to it.
These people never learn.

ADIL JUSSAWALLA

Karate

Eyes sewn, my head a bag of tricks,
I pad down streets to find my enemy.

New York London or any tall
Story I've a part in,
He is the same

White man whose daily dis–
Appearance is my brief.
Whose wars have put me on a false, if nimble
Footing. Whose tame goings–on
By day
Conceal a fratricidal fox by night.

What is it
Disproportions me of my big-time twin,
Symbiosis of loving that must kill? What pigmy
In me wants it?

I spot a giant. Call
So he won't disappear down the fatal
Error of some steps. Warn him
As he comes:

Before night
Takes in its tongue with its yellow pill,
Before day
Swallows it with a smile,
Before dawn

Breaks round his head the lights of his last
Aromatic breath,
His head will flop,
My hands will chop, then fold.

ADIL JUSSAWALLA

Approaching Santa Cruz Airport, Bombay

Loud benedictions of the silver popes,
A cross to themselves, above
A union of homes as live as a disease.
Still, though the earth be stunk and populous,
We're told it's not: our Papa'll put his nose
Down on cleaner ground. Soon to receive
Its due, the circling heart, encircled, sees
The various ways of dying that are home.
"Dying is all the country's living for,"
A doctor says. "We've lost all hope, all pride."
I peer below. The poor, invisible,
Show me my place; that, in the air,
With the scavenger birds, I ride.

Economists enclosed in History's
Chinese boxes, citing Chairman Mao,
Know how a people nourished on decay
Disintegrate or crash in civil war.
Contrarily, the Indian diplomat,
Flying with me, is confident the poor
Will stay just as they are.
Birth

Pyramids the future with more birth.
Our only desert, space; to leave the green
Burgeoning to black, the human pall,
The free
Couples in their chains around the earth.

I take a second look. We turn,
Grazing the hills and catch a glimpse of sea.
We are now approaching Santa Cruz: all
Arguments are endless now and I
Feel the guts tighten and all my senses shake.
The heart, stirring to trouble in its clenched
Claw, shrivelled inside the casing of a cage
For ever steel and foreign, swoops to take
Freedom for what it is. The slums sweep
Up to our wheels and wings and nothing's free
But singing while the benedictions pour
Out of a closing sky. And this is home,
Watched by a boy as still as a shut door,
Holding a mass of breadcrumbs like a stone.

ARUN KOLATKAR

An Old Woman

An old woman grabs
hold of your sleeve
and tags along.

She wants a fifty paise coin.
She says she will take you
to the horseshoe shrine.

You've seen it already.
She hobbles along anyway
and tightens her grip on your shirt.

She won't let you go.
You know how old women are.
They stick to you like a burr.

You turn round and face her
with an air of finality.
You want to end the farce.

When you hear her say,
"What else can an old woman do
on hills as wretched as these?"

You look right at the sky.
Clear through the bullet holes
she has for her eyes.

And as you look on,
the cracks that begin round her eyes
spread beyond her skin.

And the hills crack.
And the temples crack.
And the sky falls

with a plate-glass clatter
round the shatter-proof crone
who stands alone.

And you are reduced
to so much small change
in her hand.

ARUN KOLATKAR

Ajamil and the Tigers

The tiger people went to their king
and said, "We're starving.
We've had nothing to eat,
not a bite,
for fifteen days and sixteen nights.
Ajamil has got
a new sheep dog.
He cramps our style
and won't let us get within a mile
of meat."

"That's shocking,"
said the tiger king.
"Why didn't you come to see me before?
Make preparations for a banquet.
I'm gonna teach that sheepdog a lesson he'll never
    forget."
"Hear hear," said the tigers.
"Careful," said the queen.
But he was already gone.
Alone
into the darkness before the dawn.

In an hour he was back,
the good king.
A black patch on his eye.
His tail in a sling.
And said, "I've got it all planned
now that I know the lie of the land.

All of us will have to try.
We'll outnumber the son of a bitch.
And this time there will be no hitch.
Because this time I shall be leading the attack."

Quick as lightning
the sheepdog was.
He took them all in as prisoners of war,
the fifty tigers and the tiger king,
before they could get their paws
on a single sheep.
They never had a chance.
The dog was in fifty-one places all at once.
He strung them all out in a daisy chain
and flung them in front of his boss in one big
    heap.

"Nice dog you got there, Ajamil,"
said the tiger king.
Looking a little ill
and spitting out a tooth.
"But there's been a bit of a misunderstanding.
We could've wiped out your herd in one clean
    sweep.
But we were not trying to creep up on your
    sheep.
We feel that means are more important than ends.
We were coming to see you as friends.
And that's the truth."

The sheepdog was the type
who had never told a lie in his life.
He was built along simpler lines

and he was simply disgusted.
He kept on making frantic signs.
But Ajamil, the good shepherd
refused to meet his eyes
and pretended to believe every single word
of what the tiger king said.
And seemed to be taken in by all the lies.

Ajamil cut them loose
and asked them all to stay for dinner.
It was an offer the tigers couldn't refuse.
And after the lamb chops and the roast,
when Ajamil proposed
they sign a long-term friendship treaty,
all the tigers roared,
"We couldn't agree with you more."
And swore they would be good friends all their
    lives
as they put down the forks and the knives.

Ajamil signed a pact
with the tiger people and sent them back.
Laden with gifts of sheep, leather jackets and balls
    of wool.
Ajamil wasn't a fool.
Like all good shepherds he knew
that even tigers have got to eat sometime.
A good shepherd sees to it they do.
He is free to play a flute all day
as well-fed tigers and fat sheep drink from the
    same pond
with a full stomach for a common bond.

ARVIND KRISHNA MEHROTRA

A Letter to a Friend

I set up house while she waited
In another city; the day of our marriage
Was still far. When she saw the rooms
For the first time she said, "These
Are worse than bathrooms."
She found the walls too narrow and wanted
To run away; your mother and my aunt
Were both there when this happened.
Your mother, in her enthusiasm
And simple joy
Asked us over for lunch
When she said, "I know nothing of lunches."
It was months before things got normal again.
Anyhow, she spent her first days
With the clear sky, a few birds, the little
Interesting things which gather
Around trees; we slept in the afternoon
And awoke when the long, sad evening
Was already halfway up the window.
Kitchen smoke, the quiet smell
Of me reading in my chair, the glum
Books that smacked their tails
On the shelves like field-mice, the family
Downstairs quarrelling and crying,
Poisoned the tips of needles in her mind
And she entered an imprisoned kingdom—
A place I wouldn't touch with my bare hands.
Through two short rooms she walked
As if I were out to murder her last secret

And a blackness we all feel took hold of me;
I wanted it to, to protect myself;
Her eyes glistened, scared, scary.
At night insects on wings and feet would come
To relieve the stiff air; we played
Under the sharp moon, made little noise
Since I hardly touched her.
The first caw and the excitement
Of crows as they looked at us in bed from the
    chimney.
Bees rushed into the room, the sun pulled up,
And the girl next door wrung her underwear;
She knew I admired her ankles even in sleep.
The milkwoman brought her dog with her,
The postman came up the steps and she spent
Hours reading letters from her family,
Then wrote to each one of her brothers and
    sisters.
The lama would knock and take off his shoes
Before entering; he would hold her hand and talk
Of silence, of living in the mountains
With just enough candles to scatter the dark.
We fetched water in heavy buckets, cooked
In the open, and lying on the hillside
None thought of love.
She made tea by boiling
Water, leaves, milk and sugar
Together, adding condiments in the end;
When he left her palms were wet
And I wasn't jealous.
Across the clean, flat roofs and narrow road
Is a bare field; a camel once sat there all day,
Thin legs folded under the hump,

Looking at cows walk through trees.
So has it been.
Her blood has got more entangled in its stones
While I've kept to my lamp, beads, mirrors, jars,
A rug, pictures of purple demons,
Red, black and white ants, all sorts of fat spiders.
Three years, and I still wonder
What nakedness is, or does.
Sometimes I notice the couple next door.
It's very warm outside,
And the streets are tall and quiet.

DOM MORAES

Gone Away

My native city rose from sea,
Its littered frontiers wet and dark.
Time came too soon to disembark
And rain like buckshot sprayed my head.
My dreams, I thought, lacked dignity.
So I got drunk and went to bed.

But dreamt of you all night, and felt
More lonely at the break of day
And trod, to brush the dream away,
The misted pavements where rain fell.
There the consumptive beggars knelt,
Voiced with the thin voice of a shell.

The records that those pavements keep,
Bronze relics from the beggar's lung,
Oppress me, fastening my tongue.
Seawhisper in the rocky bay
Derides me, and when I find sleep,
The parakeets shriek that away.

Except in you I have no rest,
For always with you I am safe:
Who now am far, and mime the deaf
Though you call gently as a dove.
Yet each day turns to wander west:
And every journey ends in love.

DOM MORAES

Jason

I was the captain of my ship.
At nightfall a disquieting shape
Would eddy on the steady breeze,
Each gold curl thick and separate.
So endlessly outpoured, the fleece
Tugged at me and I followed it.

After my watch I snuffed the wick.
I was young then, I slept and woke
Wrapped in my heavy need to find.
Through the ship's planks I heard the finned
Sea monsters thrash. I dreamt of the
Fleece running wild where our wake was.
My crew and I were beardless boys
But driven by a mystery.

Our raised bows cleaved to a charred land
With breasts of salt too soft to climb.
Then I was fifty, and had found
Nothing. A bald black pilot came
And told us that the fleece was there.
I combed my beard and climbed ashore.

Small crabs tacked through the ashy sand,
Nudging their fathers' fossils and
Going nowhere always, like my want.
Then in the seawind whose white paint
Had crusted my gold curls, I ran
Where the black pilot pointed. Then,

Drunk with the sun, I wept and laughed,
That the bright fleece turned out no more
Than a burst quilt someone had left
To ooze its heart out on the shore.

A. K. RAMANUJAN

Obituary

Father, when he passed on,
left dust
on a table full of papers,
left debts and daughters,
a bedwetting grandson
named by the toss
of a coin after him,

a house that leaned
slowly through our growing
years on a bent coconut
tree in the yard.
Being the burning type,
he burned properly
at the cremation

as before, easily
and at both ends,
left his eye coins
in the ashes that didn't
look one bit different,
several spinal discs, rough,

some burned to coal, for sons

to pick gingerly
and throw as the priest
said, facing east
where three rivers met
near the railway station;
no longstanding headstone
with his full name and two dates

to hold in their parentheses
everything he didn't quite
manage to do himself,
like his caesarian birth
in a Brahmin ghetto
and his death by heart-
failure in the fruit market.

But someone told me
he got two lines
in an inside column
of a Madras newspaper
sold by the kilo
exactly four weeks later
to streethawkers

who sell it in turn
to the small groceries
where I buy salt,
coriander,
and jaggery
in newspaper cones
that I usually read

for fun, and lately
in the hope of finding
these obituary lines.
And he left us
a changed mother
and more than
one annual ritual.

GIEVE PATEL

On Killing a Tree

It takes much time to kill a tree,
Not a simple jab of the knife
Will do it. It has grown
Slowly consuming the earth,
Rising out of it, feeding
Upon its crust, absorbing
Years of sunlight, air, water,
And out of its leprous hide
Sprouting leaves.

So hack and chop
But this alone won't do it.
Not so much pain will do it.
The bleeding bark will heal
And from close to the ground
Will rise curled green twigs,
Miniature boughs
Which if unchecked will expand again
To former size.

No,
The root is to be pulled out —
Out of the anchoring earth;
It is to be roped, tied,
And pulled out — snapped out
Or pulled out entirely,
Out from the earth-cave,
And the strength of the tree exposed,
The source, white and wet,

The most sensitive, hidden
For years inside the earth.

Then the matter
Of scorching and choking
In sun and air,
Browning, hardening,
Twisting, withering,

And then it is done.

GIEVE PATEL

Servants

They come of peasant stock,
Truant from an insufficient plot.

Lights are shut off after dinner
But the city-blur enters,
Picks modulations on the skin;
The dark around them
Is brown, and links body to body,
Or is dispelled, and the hard fingers
Glow as smoke is inhaled
And the lighted end of tobacco
Becomes an orange spot.

Other hands are wide
Or shut, it does not matter
One way or other —

They sit without thought,
Mouth slightly open, recovering
From the day, and the eyes
Globe into the dim
But are not informed because
Never have travelled beyond this
Silence. They sit like animals.
I mean no offence. I have seen
Animals resting in their stall,
The oil flame reflected in their eyes,
Large beads that though protruding
Actually rest
Behind the regular grind
Of the jaws.

Africa

CHINUA ACHEBE

Public Execution in Pictures

The caption did not overlook
the smart attire of the squad. Certainly
there was impressive swagger in that
ready, high-elbowed stance; belted
and sashed in threaded dragon teeth
they waited in self-imposed restraint —
fine ornament on power unassailable —
for their cue

      at the crucial time
this pretty close-up lady in fine lace
proved unequal to it, her first no doubt,
and quickly turned away. But not
this other — her face, rigid
in pain, firmly held between her palms;
though not perfect yet, it seems
clear she has put the worst
behind her today

      in my home
far from the crowded live-show
on the hot, bleached sands of Victoria
Beach my little kids will crowd
round our Sunday paper and debate
hotly why the heads of dead
robbers always slump forwards
or sideways.

DENNIS BRUTUS

This Sun on this Rubble

This sun on this rubble after rain.

Bruised though we must be
some easement we require
unarguably, though we argue against desire.

Under jackboots our bones and spirits crunch
forced into sweat-tear-sodden slush
— now glow-lipped by this sudden touch:

— sun-stripped perhaps, our bones may later sing
or spell out some malignant nemesis
Sharpevilled to spearpoints for revenging

but now our pride-dumbed mouths are wide
in wordless supplication
— are grateful for the least relief from pain

— like this sun on this debris after rain.

DENNIS BRUTUS

Cold

the clammy cement
sucks our naked feet

a rheumy yellow bulb
lights a damp grey wall

the stubbled grass
wet with three o'clock dew
is black with glittery edges;

we sit on the concrete,
stuff with our fingers
the sugarless pap
into our mouths

then labour erect;

form lines;

steel ourselves into fortitude
or accept an image of ourselves
numb with resigned acceptance;

the grizzled senior warder comments:
"Things like these
I have no time for;

they are worse than rats;
you can only shoot them."

Overhead
the large frosty glitter of the stars
the Southern Cross flowering low;

the chains on our ankles
and wrists
that pair us together
jangle

glitter.

We begin to move
  awkwardly.

(Colesberg: en route to Robben Island)

THEO LUZUKA

The Motoka

You see that Benz sitting at the rich's end?
Ha! That motoka is motoka
It belongs to the Minister for Fairness
Who yesterday was loaded with a doctorate
At Makerere with whisky and I don't know what
Plus I hear the literate thighs of an undergraduate.

You see those market women gaping their
  mouths?
The glory of its inside has robbed them of words,
I tell you the feather seats the gold steering

The TV the radio station the gear!
He can converse with all world presidents
While driving in the back seat with his darly
Between his legs without the driver seeing a
   thing! ha! ha! ha!
Look at the driver chasing the children away
They want to see the pistol in the door pocket
Or the button that lets out bullets from the
   machine
Through the eyes of the car —
   sshhhhhhhhhhhhhhhh!
Let's not talk about it.

But I tell you that motoka can run
It sails like a lyato, speeds like a swallow
And doesn't know anyone stupid on its way
The other day I heard —
But look at its behind, that mother of twins!
A-ah! That motoka is motoka
You just wait, I'll tell you more
But let me first sell my tomatoes.

RICHARD S. MABALA

Turn-Boy

The bus squealed sluggishly to a halt
Before the bulging kanzu'd form
Of an immaculately dressed old man
Beside five jutting sacks of coconuts.

Even before the halt
Out sprang the turn-boy
Young
Ragged
Shirt fraying before the muscles on his arm.

Shikamoo Baba —
Marahaba;
And without another word
He tossed the first sack
On to his mighty shoulders
And raced to toss it once more
On to the roof of the bus.

Meanwhile
The watchful gaze of the kanzu
Never wavered
And we in the bus
Only grumbled at the delay.
The second and third sacks
Quickly followed
The fourth, a struggle
And the fifth . . . my friend
Gone was the spring

No longer did he toss
Sweat and dust streaked the ragged shirt
And straining muscles beneath
Knees faltered as the fifth sack
Was slowly heaved to his shoulders
And when he reached the ladder
And began the arduous climb
It seemed unending,
Knees shaking uncontrollably
Beneath the accumulated strain
Shoulders sagging
Mouth twisted
In a grimace of pain

And fear of failure
We watched . . .
And held our breath . . .
As the offending sack
Perched precariously on
Shaking shoulders
Teetered on the edge.
Below,
The kanzu's gaze never wavered.
Only the eyes knotted
In concern
For his coconuts
Threatened by this weakling of a turn-boy.

And inside,
While we gazed
And sighed in relief
When finally the offending load
Landed

With a thump
On the roof above our heads
We complained
And grumbled at the delay.

But one man cried out
Jamani!
That young man
So strong and lithe
Can only do this work for six months

Any longer
And his neck will be bent,
Permanently
Like a bow.
We wanted to laugh
And turned to ridicule this man of pity
Work is work
How else can the loads be lifted?
But when we turned to face the speaker
We found a man not so young,
Huge muscles decaying
Evidence of former strength
But his neck . . .
Bent like a bow.

Our mocking words stuck in our throats!

DAMBUDZO MARECHERA

Th' Anniversary

What woman is this in my arms —
And O my head an axe must have hacked.
What time, what town, what room is this —
My brain is being mangled in the meatgrinder
Of her snoring! Yesterday was th' anniversary;
On my seventh drink she appeared in strips
Of rotting flesh and faintly gleaming bones —
    Her
Hollow eye sockets instantly found me.
No electricity but dull red candles lit the scene.
We dined on worms fat as pickhandles
And she leaned on my arm as I led her on to the
    dance floor;
Thousands exhumed from mass graves danced
    with us
And thousands more soon to die applauded the
    tumult —
I remembered the time and day she and I said
    "I do", "I do"

DAMBUDZO MARECHERA

The Future A Mad Poem

The wife next door screamed all night.
The matchbox — where are the matches?
The moon is made of beans like boys
Full of might. It's all a video game.

Your mind is a motorbike exhaust pipe
Detonating fart-blasts in Cyclops's Cave.
Your ears are trees all dead bark,
I'm the rabid dog you killed last week.

Flashbacks exist only on the other side
Of the fence, where I have not been
Which is where I am. Your face of heavy rain
Drenched my history to a limp blanket.

The wolfpoem in sheepskin rhyme against ice
Screamed all night the scream lit my cigarette,
Evaporated on the spectacle I could see
How the blind grope towards red alert buttons.

CHARLES MUNGOSHI

Location Miracle

she worried herself into something
fat hostile and immovable
because of an accident in her childhood
in which she had lost an eye
and now where that eye had been
had a glaring hole:
and someone cruel had also told her
that only girls with two eyes
would get men to marry them —
so she worried some more
worried herself into something
secretive hostile and unpleasant
she worried herself beyond the point
and disintegration it looked like
she would just one day kill herself
she worried herself beyond the point
it is legal to worry any more
then just at that time we were
beginning to think we wouldn't
see her again tomorrow
a certain young man came by
this young man had one leg
and one arm
he made friends with Liza
he told her strange stories
that made her cry and laugh
at the same time
but later on the crying lessened
and the laughing worsened

they never left Liza's room
except her laugh that went
round and round the location till one day
the laugh grew wings and flew into the sky
and shook down a few stars
this young man did things as if
he had two arms and two legs
and sometimes better and he taught Liza
to do things as if she had two eyes
and when Liza could do things as if
she had more than two eyes
and her laughter could shake
down lots of stars from the sky
she became something lean, quick bright and
    lethal
and very outgoing
and so one morning she just up and left
the young man without a word
and the first man who laid eyes on her
and heard at close range her starshaking laugh
said to her why not and she said
it's you I have been waiting for all these years
and they lived happily ever after
and Liza never told him about the young man
who had taught her to laugh as if she had two
    eyes
but the young man didn't mind at all
he just went about his business as if
Liza had never happened at all

CHARLES MUNGOSHI

Sitting on the Balcony

Sitting on the balcony
fingering a glass of beer
I have bought without
any intention to drink:
I see a little boy
poking for something
in a refuse dump:
looking for a future?
I am afraid the stars say
your road leads to another
balcony, just like this one:
where you will sit
fingering a beer you have bought
without any intention to drink.

CHARLES MUNGOSHI

Two Photographs

In this one I am nineteen:
the future is still ahead.

My head, ambitiously pushed forward
into you says so: I want to get out
into the world and live.

The second one alarms me:
I am thirty, perplexedly solid
as if anchored in quicksand.

You don't see it, but I have just had
one tooth pulled out
and I can already feel the second one
starting its long journey into darkness.

My face is beginning to settle uncomfortably
into the torn-up landscape of these times.

ARTHUR NORTJE

Letter from Pretoria Central Prison

The bell wakes me at six in the pale spring dawn
with the familiar rumble of the guts negotiating
murky corridors that smell of bodies. My eyes
find salutary the insurgent light of distances.
Waterdrops rain crystal cold, my wet
face in ascent from an iron basin
greets its rifled shadow in the doorway.

They walk us to the workshop. I am eminent,
the blacksmith of the block: these active hours
fly like sparks in the furnace, I hammer metals
with zest letting the sweating muscles
forge a forgetfulness of worlds more magnetic.
The heart, being at rest, life peaceable,
your words filter softly through my fibres.

Taken care of, in no way am I unhappy,
being changed to neutral. You must decide
today, tomorrow, bear responsibility,
take gaps in pavement crowds, refine ideas.
Our food we get on time. Most evenings
I read books, Jane Austen
for elegance, agreeableness (*Persuasion*).

Trees are green beyond the wall,
    leaves through the mesh
are cool in sunshine
among the monastic white flowers of spring
    that floats

prematurely across the exercise yard, a square
of the cleanest stone I have ever walked on.
Sentinels smoke in their boxes, the wisps
curling lovely through the barbed wire.

Also music and cinema, yesterday double feature.
At four pm it's back to the cell, don't laugh
to hear how accustomed one becomes. You
    spoke
of hospital treatment — I see the smart nurses
bringing you grapefruit and tea — good
luck to the troublesome kidney.
Sorry there's no more space. But date your reply.

R. C. NTIRU

Introduction

Perhaps it was his *Ugil* shirt —
The missing button
The unassertive collar;
Perhaps it was his knotty hair
That boasted little acquaintance with the comb;
Or maybe it was his usualness
— One more impersonal handshake
Along the constant street —
That induced the functional smile
And operated the mechanical handshake.

His name didn't help either:
Mugabo Mugenge — you'd heard the name
In the out-patients' attendance queue;
Not in the current telephone directory!

You certainly needed prompting.
I said he was an old-time friend
But you continued to wave to passing cars;
I added that he was a high-placed man
And you promptly took your cue
— "A university teacher, author of several
   works" —
"Re-e-e-ally? Er — um — oh! . . . "
And you became word and emotion perfect.
Like a dog that mistakes thief for visitor
And remembers to bark at his master's coughing,
You renewed and pumped the handshake
— Reshaped your mouth to a proper smile

— Recalled his famous public talk
That you had regretfully missed . . .
And observed, thoughtfully,
How unlike his photographs he looked.

You were tuned —
Delved deep into his latest novel
And wondered why his main characters
Do not walk on the solid earth
And fail to effect living communication.
You'd have rambled on, no longer looking at
    him,
But he quipped:
"They are in good company."
And was about to add, when you knowledgeably
    interrupted,
"Society is a market stall
And men goods on display
Where the label is more important than the
    labelled
And the price more fascinating than the value."

We parted, hoping to meet again.
You went away rehearsing his name
But probably unremembering his face.

OBYERO ODHIAMBO

Betrothed

The bride, they said
had gone through school
primary secondary university upwards:
Three thousand shillings is not enough.

For having fed her
    schooled her
    employed her
Three thousand shillings is not enough —

For having borne her
    cared her
    doctored her
And "she is pure"
Three thousand shillings is not enough.

Look at her silky black hair
Darker and finer than that
Flywhisk there
Look at her forehead, a
Nice wide trace between
hairline and eyes:
"She is immensely intelligent".

Look at her eyes. Yes, look again
Two diviners' cowries spread out
symbolically on the divination mat
deep profound intelligent;
Look at those lips "ndugu" . . .

Three thousand shillings is not enough
even to shake her by the hand.

"Fathers, this is what we walked with!
Three thousand shillings
As a token of our
Love
for your daughter and you
our intended kin
It was just a token
The size of the token does not reflect
The size of the heart that bringeth it
My heart is full to the brim with
Love
for your daughter
Mine is just a token of my
Love
for her and you my intended kin."

But, young man, you say, you love
and you possibly expect love
But, young man, don't you
Don't you really feel
Three thousand shillings is not enough
even to get love?
Three thousand shillings is not enough!

GABRIEL OKARA

Adhiambo

I hear many voices
like it's said a madman hears;
I hear trees talking
like it's said a medicine man hears.

Maybe I'm a madman
I'm a medicine man.
Maybe I'm mad,
for the voices are luring me,
urging me from the midnight
moon and the silence of my desk
to walk on wave crests across a sea.

Maybe I'm a medicine man
hearing talking saps,
seeing behind trees;
but who's lost his powers
of invocation.

But the voices and the trees
are now a name-spelling and one figure
silence–etched across
the moonface is walking, stepping
over continents and seas.

And I raised my hand —
my trembling hand, gripping
my heart as handkerchief

and waved and waved — and waved —
but she turned her eyes away.

FEMI OYEBODE

Dreamtime 5

i grew up wearing my skin, without prejudice
without the unnecessary armour;
the world was easy then,
it rained hailstones, then thundered.
the hare and bullfrog, termites and their hills
the weather, were certain, and my thoughts,
fragile and wonderful, spoke a musical language;
that was long ago, before the forests collapsed
and magic retreated beyond the outskirts of my
    youth
and a curious leprosy attacked my dreams,
before myth failed to thrive in the new swamp,
in the new language, and the liturgy atrophied
in the heat and steam,
before one god shed his weariness,
and another fell ill and spellbound;
i grew up wearing my skin, without prejudice.

Dreamtime 8

i met mr boyle, oluwole boyle
last night, along moseley road,
his grey hair, dark african baritone,
his memorable face, his story touched my arm

that was before the english rain separated us,
just after his grandfather was liberated from a
    slave galley
and set free in freetown, serving dr boyle
whose name he clothed himself in
and my mother's grandfather, emancipated,
    landed
in freetown on the way to lagos,
before the stream of slaves and natives mixed
and light and coffee brushed my daughter's skin.

i met mr boyle in the hour before sleep
in the twilight chamber whose true residents are
    dead
and african and are all my relatives,
he stood beside me,
beside the flesh that are mine and separate
his grey hair, dark african baritone,
his face, the long story of our anguish,
and the unpredictable english drizzle
melted in my dream into a solitary watering hole
that final reservoir in a harsh desperate landscape,
the surprising twinkle in desmond tutu's eyes;
that was before we left him facing balsall heath,
his back to ours like oarsmen in a different time
when the cybil rescued his line and tried to
    capture his
mind.

OKOT P'BITEK

The Song of Lawino
1. I Am Not Unfair to My Husband

I am not unfair to my husband,
I do not complain
Because he wants another woman
Whether she is young or aged!
Who has ever prevented men
From wanting women?

Who has discovered the medicine for thirst?
The medicines for hunger
And anger and enmity
Who has discovered them?
In the dry season the sun shines
And rain falls in the wet season.
Women hunt for men
And men want women!
When I have another woman
With whom I share my husband,
I am glad
A woman who is jealous
Of another, with whom she shares a man,
Is jealous because she is slow,
Lazy and shy,
Because she is cold, weak, clumsy!

The competition for a man's love
Is fought at the cooking place
When he returns from the field
Or from the hunt,

You win him with a hot bath
And sour porridge.
The wife who brings her meal first
Whose food is good to eat,
Whose dish is hot
Whose face is bright
And whose heart is clean
And whose eyes are dark
Like the shadows:
The wife who jokes freely
Who eats in the open
Not in the bedroom,
One who is not dull
Like stale beer,
Such is the woman who becomes
The head–dress keeper.

I do not block my husband's path
From his new wife.
If he likes, let him build for her
An iron-roofed house on the hill!
I do not complain,
My grass–thatched house is enough for me.

I am not angry
With the woman with whom
I share my husband,
I do not fear to compete with her.

All I ask
Is that my husband should stop the insults,
My husband should refrain
From heaping abuses on my head.
He should stop being half-crazy,
And saying terrible things about my mother
Listen Ocol, my old friend,
The ways of your ancestors
Are good,
Their customs are solid
And not hollow
They are not thin, not easily breakable
They cannot be blown away
By the winds
Because their roots reach deep into the soil.

I do not understand
The ways of foreigners
But I do not despise their customs.
Why should you despise yours?

Listen, my husband,
You are the son of a Chief.
The pumpkin in the old homestead
Must not be uprooted!

KRISTINA RUNGANO

A Child's Cry

Father, remember,
You spun me thus
I never asked to be woman.

Father,
You kick me now
Talk of violation of your discipline
An asset I've fouled
This me, Father
Fruit of your loin;
I shall never forget.

We never wasted on words
Birds of separate plumage
"Females!"
You were trained to call us;
My bone-marrow is no female, Father
You see my wailing eyes
Not fountains
Don't say I'm proud
Or blame the white man's teaching
It was not he turned so long advocate
Taught honour, reputation and social security;
Is it money or cows you demand, Father?
By love I am creditor, dear sir.

No, Father
It's not our culture
It's how you've used it

Sold peace.

You see, Father
If you'd been father
Allowed relief my pregnant mind
Fury would not so pervade your centre
Feign not shock, Father
It's blood irrigates my being
You may throw furniture at my swollen belly
But Father, remember
It was you spun me thus!

KRISTINA RUNGANO

Harsh Noises

Ha
You've made good study of begging
You see the lie on my forehead
Where I scheme your fate
That's life
And yours
My luna park
That too you know
See
Your withered step
Don't open
We make loss
I'm in limbo just testing you out.

Hear
You're cheap
A prostitute
You've always said it
Always known
I'll never disagree
Never doubt your judgement.

Wait
You discard my manhood
I can't lay down the facts
What
Waste my hard-fostered calibre
Go pandanus
Lay elsewhere your sexless quivering.

I'm no monster
I don't doubt it
But you ain't worth
Even yet
A prostitute's head
Come, come
I marvel at your forgetfulness
I love my money
I love my wife
My reasons
A kick in the dust
Now I have met my creditors
Open up
I'd pee.

MONGANE WALLY SEROTE

City Johannesburg

This way I salute you:
My hand pulses to my back trouser pocket
Or into my inner jacket pocket
For my pass, my life.
Jo'burg City.
My hand like a starved snake rears my pockets
For my thin, ever lean wallet,
While my stomach groans a friendly smile to
    hunger,
Jo'burg City.
My stomach also devours coppers and papers
Don't you know?
Jo'burg City, I salute you;
When I run out, or roar in a bus to you,
I leave behind me, my love.
My comic houses and people, my dongas and my
    ever whirling dust,
My death,
That's so related to me as a wink to the eye.
Jo'burg City
I travel on your black and white and roboted
    roads,
Through your thick iron breath that you inhale,
At six in the morning and exhale from five noon.
Jo'burg City
That is the time when I come to you,
When your neon flowers flaunt from your
    electrical wind,
That is the time when I leave you.

When your neon flowers flaunt their way
    through the falling darkness
On your cement trees.
And as I go back, to my love,
My dongas, my dust, my people, my death,
Where death lurks in the dark like a blade in the
    flesh,
I can feel your roots, anchoring your might, my
    feebleness
In my flesh, in my mind, in my blood,
And everything about you says it,
That, that is all you need of me.
Jo'burg City, Johannesburg,
Listen when I tell you,
There is no fun, nothing, in it,
When you leave the women and men with such
    frozen expressions,
Expressions that have tears like furrows of soil
    erosion,
Jo'burg City, you are dry like death,
Jo'burg City, Johannesburg, Jo'burg City.

WOLE SOYINKA

Telephone Conversation

The price seemed reasonable, location
Indifferent. The landlady swore she lived
Off premises. Nothing remained
But self-confession. "Madam," I warned,
"I hate a wasted journey — I am — African."
Silence. Silenced transmission of
Pressurised good breeding. Voice, when it came,
Lipstick-coated, long gold-rolled
Cigarette-holder pipped. Caught I was, foully.
"HOW DARK?" . . . I had not misheard . . .
    "ARE YOU LIGHT
OR VERY DARK?" Button B. Button A.
    Stench
Of rancid breath of public-hide-and-speak.
Red booth. Red pillar box. Red double-tiered
Omnibus squelching tar. It *was* real! Shamed
By ill-mannered silence, surrender
Pushed dumbfoundment to beg simplification.
Considerate she was, varying the emphasis —
"ARE YOU DARK? OR VERY LIGHT?"
    Revelation came.
"You mean — like plain or milk chocolate?"
Her assent was clinical, crushing in its light
Impersonality. Rapidly, wave-length adjusted,
I chose. "West African sepia" — and as an
    afterthought,
"Down in my passport". Silence for
    spectroscopic
Flight of fancy, till truthfulness clanged her

accent
Hard on the mouthpiece. "WHAT'S THAT?"
    conceding
"DON'T KNOW WHAT THAT IS". — "Like
    brunette."
"THAT'S DARK, ISN'T IT?" — "Not
    altogether.
Facially, I am a brunette, but, Madam, you
    should see
The rest of me. Palm of my hand, soles of my feet
Are a peroxide blond. Friction, caused —
Foolishly, Madam — by sitting down, has turned
My bottom raven black — one moment,
    Madam!" — sensing
Her receiver rearing on the thunder clap
About my ears — "Madam," I pleaded,
    "wouldn't you rather
See for yourself?"

MUSAEMURA BONAS ZIMUNYA

Kisimiso

The family were gathered:
the eldest son from Bulawayo
boastful of his experiences in the city of knives
 and crooks;
one son from Harare,
a fish-pocket who can slang everyone
into ignorance with the stupefying *S'kuz'apo*
 tongue
(the family believes he is the chief mechanic at
 Lever Brothers);
a sister, latest to arrive, from Gutu
blue-painted eyelids, false eyelashes, red lips
bangles gritting in her hands
with a European hair-wig above an Ambi-proof
 face
she covers her thighs with a towel when she sits
(as for her, the family will always believe she is a
 dressmaker in Ft Vic.); the rest of the family,
 mum
 and dad, are happy to admire the latest from
 town.

Kisimiso means feasting
dozens of bread loaves, drums of tea, mountains
 of sadza,
rock-size pieces of meat of the he-goat
in lakes of thousand-eyed soup
and, of course, large pots of fizzing frothy beer.
Nothing about the book themes of good will and

155

peace
of course, good will was always here;
an old man well-known to me lost half his hair
while pulling a tourist out of a blazing car
    wreckage — in June,
six moons before last Christmas.

A child without clothes sat nodding with sleep,
his belly as big as a *muchongoyo* drum:
buzzing flies were fighting, spinning and
    tumbling
into the smelling parting between his buttocks,
Kutu, the scraggy dog was retching in front of
    him,
they ultimately gave the mother water that
had washed the madman's beard
because she could no longer leave the bush
or close her oozing behind,
and brother *s'kuz'apo*
filled the boys' hut with urine and vomit
and a powerful smell of beer gone stale.

The next day
they talked of the greatest Kisimiso
for many years.

MUSAEMURA BONAS ZIMUNYA

You Were

Ben is the one who made the claim:
the African cannot write a love poem,
he said,
And that was two years after Mrs Whitehouse
strained her back creaking from an old
    nationalist's
assault
to say we cannot write poems

And my friend, you can forget about adolescent
    boasts
I simple glared at her contemptuously.

Then I had seen Jikinya's legs
that took the blue May sun
and ravished it with fierce copper of flesh.
Human, human beauty, I screamed.

But before I had time to compose an ode
I was fuming politically
even now I still want the witch's neck.
When I had made my condemnation of her
Jikinya was a fire-place where roasting
and the death of winter were the only rituals —

and the flesh of love
was the only poem of poems
o hail the holiness of blood
that survived slavery's knife and yoke.
which the ode has not killed.

But henceforth
I will carve my jewels
from her thousand kisses
will write my songs that will sup and suck
and roll in her mirth.

INDEX OF AUTHORS